AMAZING ANIMAL MINDS

APES

by Joyce Markovics

CHERRY LAKE PRESS
Ann Arbor, Michigan

CHERRY LAKE PRESS

Published in the United States of America by Cherry Lake Publishing
Ann Arbor, Michigan
www.cherrylakepublishing.com

Reading Adviser: Beth Walker Gambro, MS, Ed., Reading Consultant, Yorkville, IL
Content Adviser: Rachel Morrison, PhD, Animal Behavior Scientist
Book Designer: Ed Morgan

Photo Credits: freepik.com, cover and title page; Courtesy of Ape Cognition & Conservation Initiative, 4; freepik.com, 5; Wikimedia Commons/William H. Calvin, PhD, 6; Wikimedia Commons/William H. Calvin, PhD, 7; freepik.com, 8; freepik.com, 9; © ZUMA Press, Inc./Alamy Stock Photo, 10; freepik.com, 11; © Asaf Weizman/Shutterstock, 12; freepik.com, 13; © Jean-Marc Bouju/AP/Shutterstock, 14; © Norma Cornes/Shutterstock, 15; freepik.com, 16; © Tristan tan/Shutterstock, 17; © Cyril Ruoso/Alamy Stock Photo, 18; freepik.com, 19; freepik.com, 20–21; © Agence Opale/Alamy Stock Photo, 22.

Cherry Lake Press is an imprint of Cherry Lake Publishing Group.

Library of Congress Cataloging-in-Publication Data has been filed and is available at catalog.loc.gov.

Printed in the United States of America by
Corporate Graphics

Note from publisher: Websites change regularly, and their future contents are outside of our control. Supervise children when conducting any recommended online searches for extended learning opportunities.

CONTENTS

KANZI THE BONOBO

In 1980, Kanzi the bonobo was born at a **primate** research center in Georgia. When Kanzi was a baby, he went to training sessions with Matata, an adult bonobo. During the sessions, scientists showed Matata lexigrams (LEX-ih-gramz) on a keyboard. A lexigram is a symbol that stands for an object or idea.

The scientists taught Matata how to use the lexigrams to communicate with them. While Matata learned, baby Kanzi played. He showed little interest in the symbols. Then one day, the small Bonobo surprised the scientists. Kanzi started using the lexigrams!

A lexigram keyboard used by Kanzi

4

Bonobos are only found in a small area in the Democratic Republic of Congo, a country in Africa.

Bonobos are sometimes called pygmy chimpanzees. They are about the same size as chimpanzees. But they have smaller heads and ears.

At first, Kanzi used the symbols to identify balls and other things. Then he communicated ideas, such as *tomorrow* and *play*. In all, Kanzi learned 500 lexigrams! And when the keyboard didn't have a symbol for something, Kanzi combined two. He pointed to "slow" and "lettuce" when he wanted kale. Why? Kale takes a long time to chew!

Kanzi the bonobo communicating with scientist Sue Savage-Rumbaugh

Scientist Sue Savage-Rumbaugh has worked with Kanzi for over 20 years. She's certain that Kanzi and other apes can understand language. They can also communicate their thoughts and feelings. Kanzi is helping Sue and other scientists uncover how apes think and the strong connection between apes and humans.

Kanzi also understands around 3,000 English words! He invents new terms, such as *potato surprise* to describe potato chips.

Kanzi showed concern for the humans he **interacted** with. If a person tripped, Kanzi told them, "Be careful!" using the keyboard.

INCREDIBLE APES

Bonobos like Kanzi belong to the ape family. Apes also include humans, gorillas, orangutans, and chimpanzees. Bonobos and chimpanzees share 98.7 percent of their **DNA** with humans! They are humans' closest living relatives.

Pictured is a chimpanzee, a kind of ape. Apes and monkeys belong to two different primate groups. The main difference is monkeys have tails. Apes do not.

"It's not a question of whether they [apes] think—it's how they think," says scientist Brian Hare. Every day, scientists are understanding more about their complex minds. So far, they have discovered that some apes use tools to get food. And apes work together for the good of their family. They also learn many skills from each other. And these are only some of their amazing abilities.

A mother mountain gorilla caring for her helpless newborn

Chimpanzees will fight and kill other chimps. Bonobos, on the other hand, settle their problems more peacefully. "Bonobos help us to see ourselves," said Frans de Waal, another scientist who studies primates.

One gorilla even learned how to talk with people! Koko the "talking" gorilla was raised by scientist Penny Patterson. Penny wanted to know what gorillas think and feel. So she taught Koko how to communicate using **American Sign Language**! The great ape was a wiz, learning a whopping 1,000 signs.

Penny holds Koko before she was fully grown. Koko also learned how to draw and paint what she saw and felt.

Koko signed to share her own thoughts and feelings. Once, after not getting the sweet juice she wanted, Koko grabbed a rubber tube. She used the tube like a straw to suck up water from a dish in her **enclosure**. Using sign language, she described herself as a "sad elephant." Koko told jokes, asked for hugs, and expressed different emotions all using sign language!

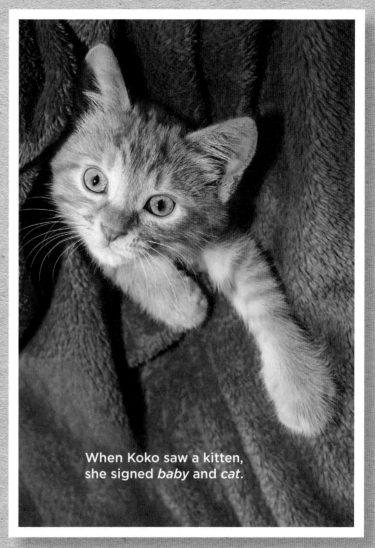

When Koko saw a kitten, she signed *baby* and *cat*.

Koko never had a baby. But she did lovingly care for several kittens, including one she named All Ball.

When most animals look in a mirror, they don't recognize themselves. In fact, they think they're looking at another animal. Yet when Koko gazed in the mirror, she made faces and picked at her teeth. Once, she even put on the lipstick that Penny had given her! She clearly recognized herself. When Penny asked Koko what she saw in the mirror, the gorilla signed, "me." "Who are you?" asked Penny. "Koko!" the gorilla replied. The ape then described herself as a "fine person gorilla."

In the wild, gorillas live together in close-knit groups called troops. They communicate with grunts and grumbles and **body language**. The gorillas work together to protect the youngest members of their troop.

The mirror self-recognition (MSR) test is a sign of self-awareness. Not all apes pass the test, but many do.

GREAT MINDS

In addition to their communication skills, apes are master tool users and makers. In the 1960s, scientist Jane Goodall first saw chimpanzees pulling leaves off twigs to make **termite**-catching tools. Before then, experts believed that only humans made and used tools.

Jane Goodall's research changed the way people understand chimps.
Here she is playing with a young chimp.

Since that time, scientists know that chimps can make and use about 20 kinds of tools. These include tools made from leaves to gather water and bandage wounds. Chimps also use long sticks to move heavy rocks, dig, and smash open beehives to get honey. A group of chimps in Gabon, Africa, makes and uses at least five different tools to collect honey!

A chimp using a stick as a tool

Chimps and other apes keep their best tools to use over and over. Sometimes, they even hide them from other apes!

At a Miami zoo, orangutans use a different kind of **technology**—iPads! The orange apes can identify and ask for things with their tablets. Keepers at the zoo say it didn't take long for the orangs to catch on. They quickly learned to point to pictures. To keep the apes engaged, the keepers gave them food choices. Now, the orangs can choose what they're having for dinner! "They're really so intelligent that I think there's no limit to what they can learn," one of the keepers said. "It's just about developing the technology to make that possible."

Orangutans, or orangs, are large apes with long, reddish hair. They often live alone and can be found on the islands of Borneo and Sumatra (see orange dots) in Southeast Asia.

Memory is another area where apes excel. The fact is many apes have better memories than people! "I've got a **PhD**. . . . You would think I could out-think an orang, and I can't," said Dan Moore, a zoo director. In one **experiment**, a human and a chimp **competed** against one another in a memory challenge. The task was recalling a series of numbers that quickly flashed across a screen.

This chimp is using a screen at the same lab in Japan where Ayuma performed his memory test.

The human, a World Memory champion, was thought to have an advantage. But Ayuma the chimp performed three times as well as the human! What explains Ayuma's amazing memory? Chimps live in dense forests where food is hard to find. Scientists believe an excellent memory may help them find food more easily.

Chimps gathering food in the wild

Chimps and orangs can remember things they experienced years ago—much like people!

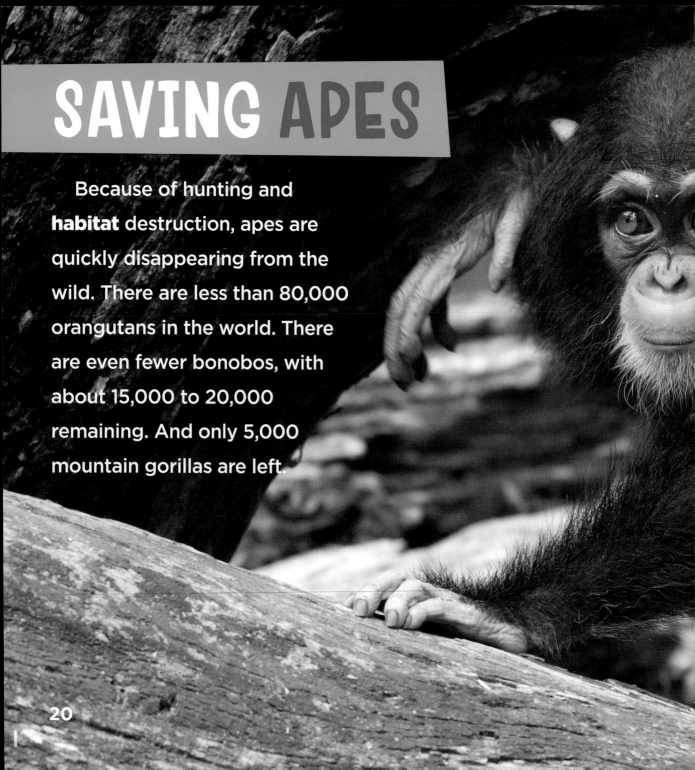

SAVING APES

Because of hunting and **habitat** destruction, apes are quickly disappearing from the wild. There are less than 80,000 orangutans in the world. There are even fewer bonobos, with about 15,000 to 20,000 remaining. And only 5,000 mountain gorillas are left.

If action isn't taken immediately, many apes could soon become **extinct**. "I think if we humans cannot save our closest relatives, then we're in really **desperate** shape," said Frans de Waal. Apes are key to understanding ourselves and where we come from. For this and many other reasons, Frans and others agree we must protect them.

Apes are some of the most playful animals. They play a variety of games together. They have been known to cover their eyes with their hands and chase each other— much like hide-and-seek!

SCIENTIST SPOTLIGHT

Frans de Waal

For almost three decades, Frans de Waal has been studying primates. He focuses his work on how chimps think, behave, and feel. Originally from the Netherlands, Frans sees a lot of similarities between humans and chimps. Like humans, chimps work to **resolve** their problems. After seeing two male chimps fight, he watched them meet on a tree, hug, and then kiss. "They depend on each other. . . . They need to fix relationships when they're broken," said Frans. The same is true for people.

Empathy is another area that interests Frans. When one chimp is upset, other chimps will hug, kiss, and groom that chimp. Chimps will also stand in silence over the bodies of their dead. "The fact that apes exist and that we can study them is extremely important and makes us reflect on ourselves," Frans said.

GLOSSARY

American Sign Language (uh-MER-uh-kuhn SINE LANE-gwij) a language that is used instead of spoken words; it is made up of hand and body movements, as well as facial expressions, and is often used by people who have difficulties hearing

body language (BOD-ee LANG-wij) a message suggested by the way an animal moves its body

competed (kuhm-PEE-tuhd) tried to win an event or contest

desperate (DESS-pur-it) something that is difficult or dangerous

DNA (DEE-EN-AY) the molecule that carries the genetic code for a living thing

empathy (EM-puh-thee) the ability to understand and share the feelings of another

enclosure (en-KLOH-zher) an area that is sealed off with a barrier, such as a fence or wall

experiment (ek-SPER-uh-ment) a scientific test set up to find the answer to a question

extinct (ek-STINGKT) when a kind of plant or animal has died out completely

habitat (HAB-uh-tat) a place in the wild where animals normally live

interacted (in-ter-ACK-uhd) acted in a way to have an effect on someone else

PhD (PEE-eych-DEE) the highest degree from a graduate school; also called a doctorate

primate (PRYE-mate) an animal in the family that includes humans, monkeys, apes, and lemurs

resolve (ri-ZOLV) to settle or find a solution to a problem or other matter

technology (tek-NOL-uh-jee) the science of making useful things

termite (TUR-mite) an insect that is like an ant and eats wood

FIND OUT MORE

BOOKS

Lloyd, Christopher. *Humanimal*. Greenbelt, MD: What on Earth Books, 2019.

Recio, Belinda. *Inside Animal Hearts and Minds*. New York, NY: Skyhorse Publishing, 2017.

Rish, Jocelyn. *Battle of the Brains: The Science Behind Animal Minds*. New York, NY: Running Press Kids, 2022.

WEBSITES

Explore these online sources with an adult:

Britannica Kids: Animal Behavior

PBS Learning Media: Animal Intelligence

PBS: The Emotional Lives of Animals

INDEX

ABOUT THE AUTHOR

Joyce Markovics has written hundreds of books for kids. She urges readers to take action to protect apes and the wild places where they live. Joyce dedicates this book to apes everywhere.